An Adoption MADE IN Heaven

AMY ANGEL GOES HOME

Kathleen Lockwood
Illustrated by Eric Bakke

Diotoma Press

Copyrighted Material

An Adoption Made in Heaven: Amy Angel Goes Home

Copyright ©2022 by Kathleen Lockwood.

Previously published in 1997 as Amy Angel Goes Home: A Heavenly Tale of Adoption.

All Rights Reserved.

No part of this publication may be reproduced, stored in a retrieval system or transmitted, in any form or by any means—electronic, mechanical, photocopying, recording or otherwise—without prior written permission from the publisher, except for the inclusion of brief quotations in a review.

For information about this title or to order other books and/or electronic media, contact the publisher:

Kathleen Lockwood/Diotima Press
BooksbyKathi.com
Kathi@booksbykathi.com

978-0-9642128-4-8 (hardcover)
978-0-9642128-5-5 (softcover)

Printed in the United States of America

Cover and Interior design: 1106 Design

Illustrated by Eric Bakke

*This book is dedicated
to my husband, Dominick,
and my children,
Trieste, Dominick, and Amelia.*

*A special thanks to Trieste
for the angel drawing
on the last page.*

"GOO-BEE-DA-BEE-DOOOO!" said the Great Guardian Angel, smiling at her class in the waiting-to-be-born heaven. The little angels and cherubs laughed. "We have to do THAT?!" exclaimed little Amy Angel.

"Yes," responded the Great Guardian Angel. "All babies talk that way. You must learn the baby ways and win three stars. Then you can be born."

O.K with me, thought Amy; I just want to go to my new home.

"GAA-BEE-DOO-BEE-DA," Amy said with a giggle. A star came swirling toward her.

TWIZZLE-TWINK

The shooting star sparkled as it landed on Amy's halo. "My first star!" Amy shouted proudly. "Two more, and I can be a real BABY!"

"O-BLA-DEE-BEE-DOO?" said Charlie.

TWIZZLE-TWINK

A bright star landed on his halo.

TWIZZLE-TWINK!

TWIZZLE-TWINK!

Shooting stars came spinning through the sky as each little angel DOO-BEE-DOOD'd, and DAA-BEE-DAA'd.

The Great Guardian Angel was pleased. "Now that you all have earned your first star," she said, "you are ready to see who your parents will be. Amy, you were first, so I'll start with you. Look over here." She waved toward the clouds below and said:

"Show me Mommy,

Show me Dad.

Amy's parents

Will soon be glad."

Instantly the clouds began to move and separate.

Amy saw two people. "These are the parents that God wants YOU to have, Amy," the Great Guardian Angel said.

Amy smiled and waved. "What's that?" she asked, pointing to a light shining from their hearts.

"That is the Light of Love," answered the Great Guardian. "It is a special love that parents have for their children. Your parents are waiting to share this love with you." Amy's heart tingled with love as she gazed at her future parents. "I love them, too," she whispered to herself.

The Great Guardian Angel turned to Charlie. She spread her arms toward the glowing clouds below and said:

*"Show me Mommy,
Show me Dad.
Charlie's parents
Will soon be glad."*

They could see two more people through the clouds. "These are the parents that God wants YOU to have, Charlie," the Angel said softly.

"Oh, thank you!" Charlie Cherub said with delight. He saw the bright white Light of Love in their hearts. He felt his love for them begin to grow.

Then he saw the soft, round Glow of Life in his mommy. He knew this Glow was the baby part of himself, growing and waiting to be born.

Meanwhile, Amy peered at her parents. *What a beautiful Light of Love my mommy and daddy have for me,* she thought as she felt love growing and connecting to them. But then, she noticed that her mommy did not have the Glow.

She turned to Charlie. "How can I be a baby if my mommy does not have the Glow?" she asked.

"I don't know," he answered, "but you don't have all your stars yet anyway, so don't worry. Your parents will be ready when you are."

Amy laughed, "I guess they'll have to be!"

Just then, the Great Guardian Angel called the class together. "It is time to learn the hic-cups," she said. "This is tricky, watch." The Great Angel bopped a little baby bounce. "Hic-CUP!"

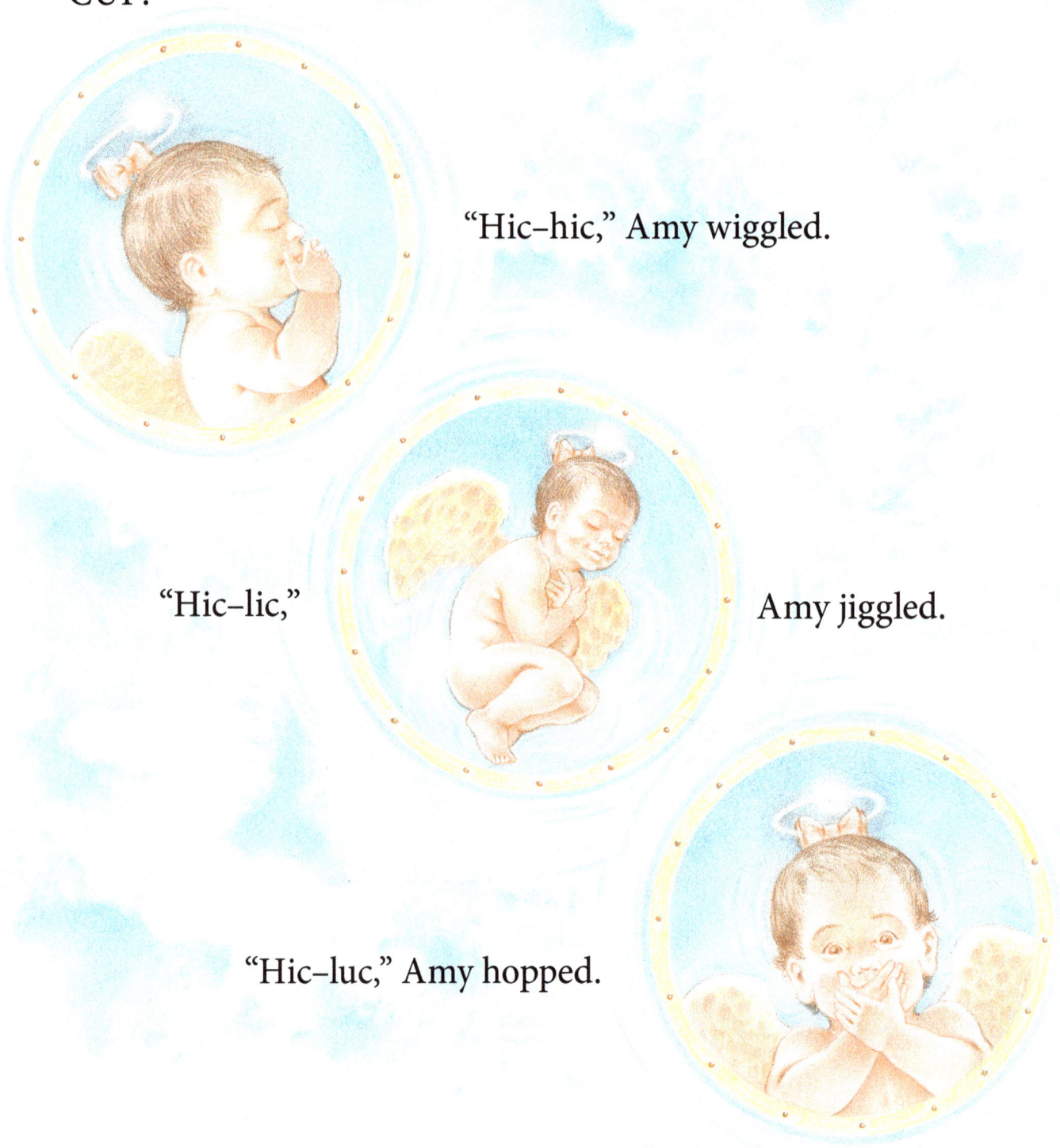

"Hic–hic," Amy wiggled.

"Hic–lic," Amy jiggled.

"Hic–luc," Amy hopped.

"Hic–CUP!" Amy bopped a perfect baby bounce.

TWIZZLE-TWINK!

Amy's star flew to her halo. She looked around.

TWIZZLE-TWINK!   TWIZZLE-TWINK!

TWIZZLE-TWINK!

A blizzard of stars fell as each little baby-to-be bopped a perfect baby bounce with a "Hic-CUP!" Now all the little angels had two stars.

"You must be tired from all the wiggles and jiggles and hopping and bopping," the Great Guardian Angel said. "It's time for a practice nap."

The angels flew to their favorite clouds. Charlie settled on a huge Tyrannosaurus rex. Amy sat on the back of a giant eagle. Watching their parents was much more fun than sleeping.

"My mommy and daddy are getting ready for me right now," Charlie said. "Look at my new bed and the big teddy bear!"

Amy peeked through the clouds. "MY parents are getting ready for me too," she said. "See how they're holding my blanket? I just know they're thinking about me." She could feel their love drawing her closer and closer to them.

The Great Guardian called the class together again. "This is the final lesson, and the most important one," she said. "As a newborn baby, you won't be able to talk. But your parents will know how much you love them when you do the Silent Squeeze. Now, think loving thoughts, hold your partner's finger, and SQUEEZE!"

Amy held Charlie's finger and squeezed. TWIZZLE-TWINK! Down flew her star.

Charlie held Amy's finger and squeezed. TWIZZLE-TWINK! Down flew his star.

TWIZZLE-TWINK!

TWIZZLE-TWINK!

TWIZZLE-TWINK!

In a lightning flash, all the angels had their third star.

"Congratulations!" the Great Guardian Angel said to all her happy students. "Now you are ready to be born!" The class cheered as they flew to watch their parents from heaven one last time.

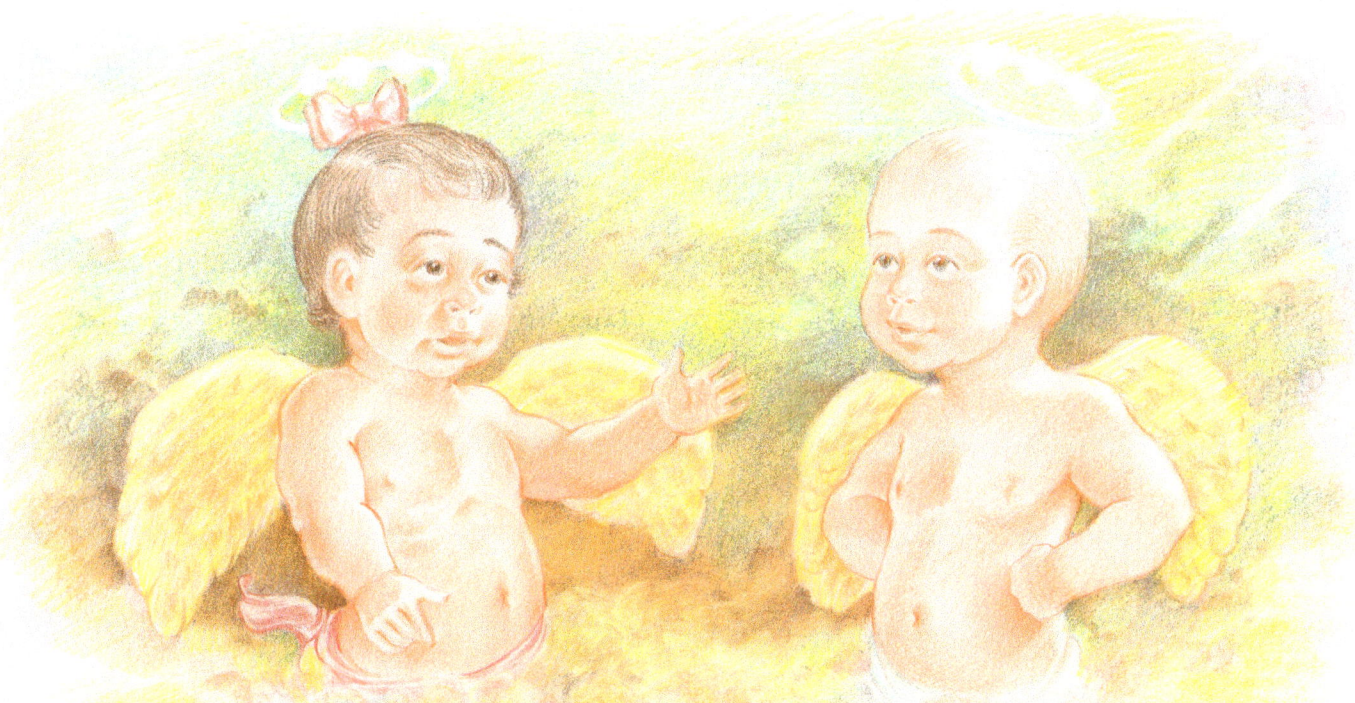

Amy Angel looked at her mommy and daddy again. Her heart beamed with love for them. "Still no Glow in my mommy," she said to Charlie. "I'm ready to be a baby now, but how can I ever be born if my mommy doesn't have the Glow?" She was so worried that she began to cry.

The Great Guardian Angel heard her question and came to help.

"Great Guardian," Amy angel sighed, "I have all my stars, and I am ready to be born, and my parents are ready for me too! Their Light of Love is so bright! But my mommy doesn't have the Glow. How will I ever be a baby?"

"Don't worry, Amy," comforted the Great Angel. "You will be in your parents' arms soon. Your mommy and daddy have been praying for your arrival for a long time, and God has a Special Friend who will help you get to your parents."

"God's Special Friend helping me?" Amy began to smile.

"Yes, you are going to be adopted, and this makes you a very special baby, too. Look here." The Great Guardian Angel raised her hand and said:

Show me the one with LOVE so dear, to be God's helper for Amy here.

The clouds parted.

As they peeked through the clouds, the Great Guardian Angel smiled at Amy and said, "There is your birth mother, and she has your Glow. She is God's Special Friend, and she will deliver you to your parents."

Amy Angel was pleased with God's plan for her. "I'll be home soon," she whispered with a smile.

"Yes, but right now, it is time for Charlie to go," the Great Guardian Angel proclaimed.

She brought them through a long tunnel of clouds to the sky-train station. Charlie boarded a big blue train with shining diamond wheels. He excitedly waved goodbye to his friends. Bright sparks flew from the train as it carried Charlie home.

Amy Angel looked up at the Great Guardian. "Do I get on the train now, too?" she asked.

"Amy, you are to be adopted, so you will go to your parents in a different way," responded the Great Guardian Angel. "You are going by boat."

"A boat or a train…I don't care *how* I get there. I just want to go HOME," Amy replied.

She turned and saw the huge white sails of a beautiful ship, with hundreds of angels dancing around it.

"Are they having a party?" she asked.

"Yes, Amy. This is YOUR special birthday party. Your parents have waited a long time for you. When you arrive, their joy will be so great that their hearts will burst with their love for you.

Sparks of love will fly everywhere. These angels want to share that special joy of your parents' love.

"I'm ready!" cried Amy with delight.

She settled into the sailboat, and the gentle rocking of the ship soon turned her happy thoughts into beautiful dreams.

When Amy awoke, she was in her mommy's arms. She felt the love pouring from her parents' hearts. It covered her with warm, beautiful feelings.

I'm home! she thought as she saw tears of joy in her parents' eyes.

She saw sparks of love fly up into the heavens. Joyful angels played in their light.

I want my parents to know that I love them too, Amy thought. Remembering the Great Guardian Angel's last lesson, she squeezed her daddy's finger…and he smiled.

Years later, Amy thought she remembered…

Thank you for reading and sharing this. I hope that you enjoyed it, found it heartwarming and that it facilitated a conversation with you and your child.

You might be interested in a brief backstory about what motivated me to write this book.

> One late September afternoon in 1995, my son walked through the front door, dropped his lunch bag on the foyer floor, and ran up to his room without his usual visit to the kitchen for a snack.
>
> I followed him, wondering what happened in kindergarten that day. He wouldn't eat; he was pouting. I asked him, "What is wrong? What happened in school today?"
>
> I finally got my answer: "Jenny told me that you are not my real mommy," he blurted out with a loud sob.
>
> "Of course, I'm real," I answered in shock. Seeds for the Amy Angel story were planted that afternoon and nurtured during our conversations over the next few months.
>
> Our two daughters were born between multiple miscarriages. Soon after one such loss, my son's birth mother walked into my husband's law office asking him to find a loving home for her soon-to-be-born child. We felt chosen. Sometimes I wondered, why were we gifted with *these* children?
>
> Ultimately, I understood that a Divine Hand must be at play.
>
> *An Adoption Made in Heaven* was written to let all children know that they are exactly where they belong, and home is where they are loved.

Online reviews validate that our work matters, and favorable five-star reviews are the number one reason people decide to buy a book. So please take a few minutes to share what this book has meant to you and your child.

A gift of a rich thought is like giving as the angels give.

Please know how much I appreciate that, and I hope this book has an enduringly positive impact on you and your loved ones.

I am available for book clubs, presentations, and podcasts; please send all requests to *kathi@booksbykathi.com*.

Please look for my recent books, *A Christmas Eve Adventure: Finding the Light of the World* and *The King and the Monster*.

—Rev. Kathleen Lockwood

www.ingramcontent.com/pod-product-compliance
Lightning Source LLC
Chambersburg PA
CBHW061817290426
44110CB00026B/2897